INHALE

CONFIDENCE

EXHALE

DOUBT

INHALE CONFIDENCE, EXHALE DOUBT

Inhale Confidence, Exhale Doubt

(A Guide to Redefining ...YOU)

Share This Inspiration to

EMPOWER, UPLIFT, AND TRANSFORM

KIMBERLY GAIL SAUNDERS

INHALE CONFIDENCE, EXHALE DOUBT

Dedication:

"To the mothers around the world who inhale confidence with every breath, letting it fill their lungs and strengthen their spirits. May you forever exhale doubt, releasing it to the winds, and in its place, may you cultivate a garden of self-assurance and empowerment. This book is dedicated to your journey of blossoming into the powerful and fearless individuals you are meant to be."
I was once you... *Kimberly Gail*

**To my daughter Aigner and my son Stephen, and all my Amazing, Incredible Grandchildren with All My Love...* ♥

INHALE CONFIDENCE, EXHALE DOUBT

WELCOME

"Inhale Confidence, Exhale Doubt"
(A Guide to Redefining YOU)

THANK YOU for being here. You are about to embark on a transformative journey—one that will inspire you to embrace your true potential, shatter self-doubt and cultivate unshakable assurance. As you turn the pages, you'll discover a wealth of wisdom, practical advice, and inspirational stories that will help you unlock the incredible power that resides within you. Get ready to inhale confidence and exhale doubt because your journey to a more empowered you starts now. No more being lost amongst the many titles of life. This Ends Today!

www.KimberlyGailspeaks.com

This guide is meant to be interactive so you can personalize and implement daily… Enjoy

~ Kimberly Gail

CONTENTS

DISCOVERING YOUR AUTHENTIC IDENTITY: *"WHO AM I?"* 14

CULTIVATING THE GARDEN OF CONFIDENCE: *"BUILD YOUR CONFIDENCE MUSCLE"* 26

EMBRACE THE POWER OF YOUR OWN HAPPINESS: *"THE PERMISSION YOU'VE BEEN WAITING FOR"* 38

DISSOLVING THE SHACKLES OF SELF-DOUBT: *"WHAT'S THE DOUBT ABOUT?"* 45

DISCOVERY JOURNEY: *"YOUR LIFE'S PURPOSE"* 55

NAVIGATING LIFE'S JOURNEY: *"STAYING ENGAGED WITH YOUR TRUE SELF"* .. 60

UNLEASH YOUR INNER POWER: *"THE ART OF SHOWING UP"* 67

SETTING YOURSELF FREE: *"NO TURNING BACK"* 73

JUST A LITTLE SOMETHING... 78

CONCLUSION 82

NOW IS THE TIME... 86

INHALE CONFIDENCE, EXHALE DOUBT

INHALE CONFIDENCE, EXHALE DOUBT

DOES THIS LOOK FAMILIAR?

Discovering Your Authentic Identity:
"WHO AM I?"

Have you ever pondered the depths of your identity? Beyond the titles of mother, wife, daughter, businesswoman, athlete, and more – lies the essence of "you." These roles, though vital, can sometimes engulf your true self. When did you last connect with the person within these labels? Unveiling "Who am I?" is a labyrinthine quest, made complex by the societal roles we fill.

Our identities amalgamate interests, experiences, traits, choices, values, and beliefs. This kaleidoscope defines us. Once you go through your transformation, a crystal-clear comprehension illuminates the path to informed decisions and a self-created life.

**Defining Your Core Values & Beliefs:

Picture life like a house; without a robust foundation, it crumbles. Core values guide us, resembling a compass. Through them, we fashion a personal philosophy, directing our decisions, actions, and demeanor. Once embraced, these values mold an envisioned life. Once you understand your values and beliefs, you can build a life you want with a strong foundation.

**Embracing Growth, Evolution, and Change:

Identity isn't stagnant; it morphs with experiences. Shed misconceptions – you aren't confined to your past. To align with your purpose, adaptability is key. Reinvent yourself, tailoring aspirations to match your growth. As the chapters of your life unfold, embrace renewal, refocus, and reclaim your path.

**Changing Your Environment, Not Your Essence:

Environment shapes us profoundly. Friends, family, community, and work wield transformative power. Embrace change as an ally. Shift your surroundings to harmonize with your values. Encompassing yourself with kindred spirits fosters growth. Alteration births authenticity.

Authenticity emanates from within – untethered by external judgment. Meaningful bonds bloom when actions mirror core values. Self-belief molds authenticity. By recognizing your inner landscape, you assert your identity confidently. Stand resolute in self-awareness.

Finding your identity is a deeply personal and often ongoing journey. It's about understanding who you are, what you value, and what makes you unique.

Here are some steps and considerations that might help you in this process:

1. <u>Self-Reflection</u>: Take time to reflect on your thoughts, feelings, desires, and experiences. Consider what makes you happy, what your strengths and weaknesses are, and what activities or interests bring you fulfillment.

**_____
_____
_____
_____
_____

2. <u>Explore Your Passions</u>: Engage in activities that genuinely interest you and help you better communicate your thoughts and emotions. Exploring different hobbies, interests, and creative pursuits can help you uncover aspects of yourself that you might not know. What do you truly enjoy? Why? How often do you engage in this activity?

**_____
_____
_____
_____
_____

3. <u>Personal Values</u>: Identify your core values. What principles and beliefs are most important to you? Personal growth, compassion, empathy, or service and giving. What's important to you? Aligning your life with your values can provide a strong sense of purpose and identity.

** _____
_____
_____
_____
_____
_____

4. <u>Life Experiences</u>: Reflect on your life experiences, both positive and negative. They contribute to shaping who you are. Consider how you've grown and changed as a result of these experiences. What are some of your positive changes and what can you do better?

** _____
_____
_____
_____
_____
_____

5. <u>Cultural and Family Background</u>: Your cultural and family background can play a significant role in shaping your identity. Explore your heritage, traditions, and the values instilled by your family. Share a value or tradition to reflect on and how it impacts your sense of self.

** _____
_____
_____
_____
_____
_____

6. <u>Personal Relationships</u>: The people you surround yourself with can influence your identity. Reflect on how your relationships impact your sense of self and whether they align with who you want to be. Who are your people? And why do you choose them?

** _____
_____
_____
_____
_____
_____

7. <u>Mindfulness and Meditation</u>: Practicing mindfulness and meditation can help you connect with your inner thoughts and feelings. These practices can also promote self-awareness and a deeper understanding of yourself. What mindfulness practices resonate with you? Walking, art, exercising, journaling, Yoga, or maybe a special place?

** _____
_____
_____
_____
_____
_____

8.   <u>Challenges and Growth</u>: Welcome challenges and setbacks—they're growth opportunities, revealing your resilience and capabilities. What's your current toughest challenge? And what are you doing to address it?

** _____
_____
_____
_____
_____
_____

9.   <u>Seeking Guidance</u>: Consider talking to a therapist, counselor, or life coach. Professional guidance can help you navigate your thoughts, feelings, and experiences in a supportive environment. Have you ever sought therapy? What was it like for you? If you have never tried therapy, would you be open to it? If not, what is the barrier?

** _____
_____
_____
_____
_____
_____
_____

10. <u>Travel and Exploration</u>: Traveling and experiencing new cultures can broaden your perspective and challenge your existing beliefs, allowing you to discover new facets of your identity. If you could go anywhere, where would it be? Is this a possibility for you in the future?

**_____
_____
_____
_____
_____

11. <u>Continuous Learning</u>: Engage in lifelong learning. The more you learn about different subjects and perspectives, the more well-rounded and informed your identity can become. What would you be interested in learning and why? How can you continue this process?

**_____
_____
_____
_____
_____

12. <u>Embrace Change</u>: Remember that your identity is not fixed. It can evolve over time as you learn, grow, and have new experiences. Embrace change as a natural part of your journey. What change will you embrace now?

** _____
_____
_____
_____
_____
_____

13. <u>Journaling</u>: Keeping a journal can help you track your thoughts, feelings, and experiences over time. It can serve as a valuable tool for self-discovery. "Could you share a positive recognition you've made about yourself recently?"

** _____
_____
_____
_____
_____
_____

14.　<u>Be Patient</u>: Finding your identity is a process that takes time. Be kind with yourself and allow the journey to unfold naturally. "Reflect on the ways in which you've exercised your patience or how you can begin to do so."

**_____
_____
_____
_____
_____
_____

Remember, there is no one-size-fits-all approach to finding your identity. It's a unique journey for each individual. Embrace the process and allow yourself the space to discover and redefine who you are over time.

In conclusion, navigating "Who am I?" necessitates soul-searching, core value exploration, and the audacity to metamorphose. Allow your identity to flourish, evolving through experiences. Harness your environment to enhance authenticity. In knowing "you," relationships deepen, self-expression flows, and your true essence radiates unencumbered.

At this point, look back on your responses and journal about what you are thinking: Does this journey seem possible?

A reminder: ***"I AM AN OVERCOMER"***

INHALE CONFIDENCE, EXHALE DOUBT

INHALE CONFIDENCE, EXHALE DOUBT

INHALE CONFIDENCE, EXHALE DOUBT

"USE YOUR MUSCLE"

Cultivating the Garden of Confidence: *"Build Your Confidence Muscle"*

Just as we tirelessly strengthen our physical muscles, isn't it time we gave our confidence muscle the attention it deserves? Confidence, the mental muscle, requires training just like the body. Amidst discussions on self-love and assurance, building confidence often remains in the shadows. My personal transformation unveiled the power within, turning insecurities into empowerment. I began nurturing my self-confidence by initiating a shift in my mind set by using mental disciplines. This transformation enabled me to elevate my thinking and approach situations with a more deliberate and thoughtful perspective while paving my path toward personal growth. I embrace, the truth that confidence is a self-crafted masterpiece. Imagine the limitless possibilities that await you by cultivating this precious trait.

**Nurturing Your Mind with Declarations:

Plant the seeds of self-belief through declarations. Affirmations like "I am worthy," "I am powerful and creative," and "Confidence is my second nature" are more than words –they're the water and sunlight your self-assuredness craves.
Let these mantras shape your daily reality, for consistency begets transformation. Doing this I created a reliable and sustainable pattern of actions and behaviors that work; repetition reinforced my neutral pathways in my brain, making things easier to perform. Being consistent played another key role, over time my small incremental improvements accumulated, resulting in significant changes.
"I crafted personalized affirmations designed to fortify my inner

self and immersed myself in meditation to truly feel their impact. I intentionally sought out situations that instilled feeling of worthiness, empowerment, capability, strength, and a sense of accomplishment within me." In this chapter are 20 daily affirmations to start your journey.

****Dress as a Manifestation of Confidence:**

Apparel isn't just fabric; it's an emblem of your self-image. Dressing confidently orchestrates an energy shift, resonating across life's facets. Embrace attire as a tool of empowerment, inspiring a more purposeful existence. Watch as your aura brightens, interactions become warmer, and compliments cascade like confetti. Consciously curate your attire, asking, "What would the Confident me wear today?" Embrace this sartorial journey towards authenticity.

    I was the one who grabbed the sweats or tights to head out daily with clothes to wear in the closet. Didn't realize I was doing the same thing day after day (I believe they call that insanity.) Until one day my granddaughter said: hey Mom-Mom, where did you go today? you look nice. This was the day I decided to do something different no sweats today, I styled my hair, put on a little make up on and shifted my energy and there was the new me.

    It made me realize that if she could express so much complimentary enthusiasm with just a simple pair of jeans, a cute top and of course my hair was looking sharp. What might have she been holding back all those times when she said nothing at all?

I must confess that I experienced a wonderful sense of well-being on that particular day. It inspired me to elevate my daily energy and maintain the same positive feeling. I begin to remember that I like to not only feel good but look good as well. It served as a significant confidence boost for me, and I embraced the change.

**Crafting Joy as a Confidence Architect:

Amid life's chaos, carve sanctuaries of joy. Pause, indulge, and embrace passions that resonate. This practice enhances your self-confidence ecosystem. In the art of creating joy, you assume the role of an architect, designing a life that fosters fulfillment. Whether sharing meals with friends, basking in family moments, strolling along nature's pathways, or immersing in captivating books – each stitch in this fabric of joy weaves a stronger sense of self. "By prioritizing yourself, you're not leaving your family behind; instead, you're acknowledging your own importance and becoming an integral part of the family's well-being."
When you can do this, you become a better person overall. My favorite is "Game Night!" ... *Bingo* anyone?

As you delve into the intricacies of building confidence, remember that it's not a destination, but a journey. Nourish your confidence garden with patience and dedication. Just as a garden flourish with care, your confidence blossoms with time and consistency.
Engage in these practices earnestly and watch the tapestry of your life weave threads of authenticity, empowerment, and fulfillment. You hold the brush to paint your canvas of confidence, so wield it boldly! Our bodies grow stronger with deliberate effort, yet we often neglect our confidence muscle. Just as physical prowess requires training, so does our mental resilience. This intangible yet potent trait can be nurtured. While discussions about self-love abound, the journey of building self-assurance remains uncharted.

My transformation began internally, turning insecurities into empowerment. Embracing self-responsibility led to a life-altering shift. Confidence is a self-crafted masterpiece that holds profound potential. Personally, I initiated the process of reintroducing joy into my life by engaging in a daily activity that brought me pleasure. Initially, I returned to the gym, not for a strenuous workout, but simply to unwind in the jacuzzi. Gradually, I incorporated leisurely walks on the track and joined a few fitness classes. It was only after this that I felt prepared to venture into the weight room to enhance my overall physical strength.

Through this journey, I came to recognize that I was devoting time to something exclusively for my own well-being, and I found genuine enjoyment in the experience.

INHALE CONFIDENCE, EXHALE DOUBT

<u>Initiate Your Confidence Journey & Strengthen Your Mind to amplify your self-worth:</u>

- **"I am worthy"**
- **"My confidence is expanding"**
- **"I am powerful and creative"**
- **"I am sculpting a better life"**
- **"Courage courses through me"**
- **"Gratitude fuels my days"**
- **"Productivity is my ally"**
- **"Resilience defines me"**
- **"Energetic and potent, I stand"**
- **"Confidence flows within me"**

Elevate these affirmations into your daily ritual, embedding them in your essence. Consistency will yield transformation.

In conclusion, sculpting your confidence muscle is an art, requiring daily cultivation. Yes, you may have setbacks but staying the course is key. I'm living proof that it can be done. Affirmations shape your mindset; clothing empowers; joy anchors you. The voyage towards self-assurance involves purposeful choices that resound with authenticity. In this tapestry of discovery, bask in the radiance of your strengthened self, ready to embrace life's expanse with newfound certainty.

A reminder: ***"I AM STRONG"***

INHALE CONFIDENCE, EXHALE DOUBT
Daily declarations to boost your mood and mindset:

1. I am worthy of love, success, and happiness.
2. I believe in my abilities and trust in my journey.
3. Today, I choose positivity and let go of negativity.
4. I am resilient and can overcome any challenge that comes my way.
5. Every day is a new opportunity for growth and learning.
6. I radiate confidence and attract positive energy into my life.
7. I am grateful for all the blessings in my life, big and small.
8. I am in control of my thoughts and can create my reality.
9. I embrace change and welcome new experiences with an open heart.
10. I deserve success and I can achieve my goals.
11. I am at peace with my past and excited for my future.
12. I am kind to myself and practice self-care regularly.
13. I am surrounded by supportive and loving people who uplift me.
14. I am deserving of abundance and prosperity in all areas of my life.
15. I trust the universe to guide me towards my highest good.
16. I release all doubt and replace it with unwavering faith in myself.
17. I am a magnet for positivity, attracting joy and happiness effortlessly.
18. I am in tune with my intuition and make choices that align with my purpose.
19. I am a work in progress, and I embrace my journey with patience and grace.
20. I am unique and valuable, and I contribute positively to the world around me.

Ready For Your BOOST!!!

Now it's your turn! Write down your personal declarations **Add, Believe, **Read,** <u>*then*</u> **Implement**!
(Get set, on your mark, get your Pen and **START!**) … "might be a little corny but I like it!"

Remember, repeating your declarations daily and truly believing in them can help shift your mindset towards a more positive and empowered outlook on life. Place them all around you as reminders.

A reminder: ***"I AM FABULOUS"***

INHALE CONFIDENCE, EXHALE DOUBT

INHALE CONFIDENCE, EXHALE DOUBT

Embrace the Power of Your Own Happiness: *"The permission you've been waiting for"*

In a world that's often awash with chaos and uncertainty, there's one thing that remains steadfastly within your control: your happiness. So, I'm here to remind you that there's no need to wait for someone else to grant you the permission to be happy; that power lies within you, and it's time to unleash it in all its glory.

**The Myth of External Permission

Let's get one thing straight right off the bat - the idea that happiness requires external validation is a fallacy. Happiness is not a gift bestowed by others, but a treasure you grant upon yourself. You hold the key to your own joy, and it's high time you used it.
Yet so many of us find ourselves trapped in a cycle of waiting for that elusive "permission" from someone else, be it a boss, a partner, or society at large.
We sit and hope for a nod of approval before we can finally declare ourselves as happy. But here's the kicker: that approval is nothing more than a mirage, a phantom shackle that holds us back from our own inner bliss.

No one can force you to be happy, nor can they force you to do anything you don't wish to do. The only permission that truly matters is the one you reward yourself. So, why wait any longer? Give yourself permission to be happy!"

**Permission for Acceptance

Acceptance is the first step towards happiness. It doesn't mean you have to surrender your desires or give up on your dreams. It simply means acknowledging where you are right now and finding contentment in the present moment. Life is a swirling blend of moments, some sweet and others bitter, but happiness isn't about having everything you want; it's about making peace and embracing what you have.

The essence of happiness lies in the alignment of your thoughts, words, and actions. When these elements harmonize, you'll find yourself in a state of pure joy. Give yourself permission to embrace acceptance and let the symphony of happiness play on.

**Permission to Be Imperfect

Perfection is an illusion, a mirage that leads us astray from the path to happiness. In a world filled with complexities and uncertainties, imperfection is not a flaw but a badge of authenticity. It's time to wear your imperfections proudly, for they are what make you unique. Don't let societal pressures dictate who you should be or how you should act. Instead, trust your inner compass, that gut feeling that guides you towards your true self. Avoid becoming entangled in the illusion of judgment through social media platforms. You don't require them to belong. Always keep this in mind. Perfectionism is a joy-stealer. It robs you of the happiness that comes from embracing your quirks and idiosyncrasies. So, toss perfectionism out the window and watch as happiness blossoms in its place.

**Permission to Keep the Blues Away

Emotions are the colors that paint the canvas of our lives, and sometimes, the palette includes blues. But remember, your emotions do not define you entirely. Just as the sun always rises after the darkest night, your positive thoughts can illuminate your path. When you're focused on positivity, amazing things start happening.

The blues are not your captors; they are visitors. Acknowledge them, but don't let them overstay their welcome. Choose to see the shades of blue as beautiful, just as they are. Prioritize your well-being by engaging in activities that bring you joy and surrounding yourself with people who make your heart sing.

**<u>Permission to Choose</u>

In the quest to please others, we often forget to please ourselves. The art of choosing for oneself is a powerful source of happiness. So, take a moment to reflect on your desires and dreams. What do you truly want? Once you've uncovered your heart's desires, have the courage to make choices that align with your inner compass. Be sure to establish boundaries with those who may drain your energy.
Happiness is not a passive state; it's an active choice. It's a decision to prioritize your own well-being and happiness over external expectations.

**<u>Permission to Act</u>

Happiness is not solely a matter of inborn temperament. While some may have a natural disposition towards joy, true happiness comes from taking
deliberate actions. The happiest people aren't those with the best of everything; they are those who make the best of everything they have and those who practice self-care.

So, what actions can you take right now, with your own permission, to set yourself free? Happiness is a journey, and it begins with you granting yourself the authority to embark upon it.

*Remember this: the permission to be happy is a gift you give yourself. It's a powerful declaration that you are the captain of your own joy. So, seize it with both hands, and let the world witness the radiant happiness that you create for yourself. Embrace the power of your own happiness, for it's a treasure that only you can unlock, and the world is waiting to see you shine. Let's leave the validations for the parking tickets.
A reminder: *"I AM DESERVING"*

LOVE YOURSELF

INHALE CONFIDENCE, EXHALE DOUBT

Dissolving the Shackles of Self-Doubt: *"What's the Doubt about?"*

Self-doubt, a universal visitor, can emerge as we venture into the unknown, be it new jobs, tests, or challenges. Yet, what if we could tame, this unwelcome guest? Self-doubt, characterized by uncertainty about oneself, might be common, but it's not invincible.

Allow me to guide you through my journey of grappling with self-doubt and emerging fortified. Five years ago, my life took an unexpected turn. I went from being a grandmother to six beautiful children to becoming the primary caregiver for four of them. It wasn't a tragedy that brought about this change, but it had a profound impact on my life. At that time, I was happily living with my best friend, dealing with minimal bills, and feeling pretty content. I even had dreams of a trip to Paris in the works.

But suddenly, I found myself searching for a new place to live in the suburbs, close to their school, and starting a new chapter in life. Paris had to be put on hold indefinitely.

I began to worry about the emotional, physical, and mental well-being of not just myself, but my grandchildren too. Self-doubt crept in, and I questioned if I could handle this. I had already raised two adults, and now I was starting over with four more. I remember praying and meditating a lot during those days, asking the Lord if this was truly where I was meant to be. And let me tell you, my grandchildren ranged from starting kindergarten to 6th grade, so it was quite a range of needs to address.

But I quickly realized that I couldn't afford to dwell in self-doubt. There was too much to do. So, I fast-forwarded to the present, and I can confidently say that embracing this new reality was the best decision I ever made. It all started with a shift in my mindset.

Instead of hiding my struggles, I began asking for help in my new environment. I had to realize and believe that I was not alone and when I opened my eyes to this reality, I received an incredible amount of support from my amazing community, and I am forever grateful to all of them.

Today, my grandchildren are in 5th, 8th, 10th, and 12th grades, with three of them set to graduate this year. What an accomplishment, and it only gets better with each passing season. Breaking free from the chains of self-doubt wasn't always easy, but it was an incredible journey of growth and resilience. I wouldn't trade this learning experience for anything in the world.

<u>A Confluence of Indecision and Realization</u>:

We've all stood at the crossroads of uncertainty. I too have weathered indecisiveness, fearing erroneous choices. But that couldn't be my narrative. The realization dawned that this trajectory wasn't ordained for me, and I could imagine this story in a way that will be beneficial to my well-being. Doubt and its sinister accomplice, fear, hinder growth and potential. Fueled by determination, I embarked on a quest to dismantle self-doubt's fortress. I made a conscious choice to prioritize mental clarity and unwavering focus while removing any obstacles from my life. I'm not going to say it was an easy task. So, I integrated prayer, meditation, and self-belief techniques, cultivating the belief that my desired life outcomes were unfolding in the present moment.
Whenever negativity surfaced, I harnessed the strength of my mental discipline to swiftly transition to positive thoughts and actions.

Don't let self-doubt run your show. Crush it and gain total confidence! It's the mindset change that will get you through and keep you going.

Rebuilding Trust:

Embrace self-compassion, a cornerstone of trust-building. Picture this: start and end each day with affirmations, seven reflective declarations. Crafted to your resonance, they uplift:
- "I wake up content with myself daily"
- "Initiative propels my decisions"
- "Fear wields no dominion over me"
- "I demand nothing less than my worth"
- "My goals are within grasp"
- "I trust my judgement"
- "Self-love and kindness are my beacons"

With seven symbolizing a sense of completion, it's time to formulate your seven Declarations.

Resurrecting from Past Achievements:

Past successes validate your potential. Use self-reflection, as a potent tool, it isn't about dwelling on failure or success but gleaning insights from your experience's. Extract the lessons from your history to bolster your present. Redirect your focus from past mishaps to present growth, as each moment shapes the tapestry of your identity.

The Peril of Comparison:

Self-doubt thrives when contrasted with others' achievements. Abandon this futile pursuit. Instead, nurture self-focus, a conduit to joy and success. Divert energy from comparing to enriching your unique journey. While social media can serve as a valuable tool, it can

also foster feelings of comparison and self-doubt. It's important to establish clear boundaries and adhere to them to mitigate these negative effects.
You define You!

****Cultivating a Supportive Circle:</u>

You needn't navigate this odyssey alone. Forge alliances with those who uplift, energize, and kindle your growth. Detach from the energy-drainers; associate with those who share your aspirations. Mutual nourishment fuels a synergy of self-improvement. Participating in different clubs or organizations, such as a book club or a mom's group, can be a great way to connect with others. Enjoying a night out or engaging in partner workouts not only helps you stay accountable but also adds an element of enjoyment to your activities.
A reminder: *"I AM POWERFUL"*

13 Self-Doubt Dismantling Tips:

Dismantling self-doubt is a crucial step toward building self-confidence and achieving your goals.

1. **Recognize It:* Awareness is the first step. Acknowledge when self-doubt creeps in, and don't try to ignore or suppress it. Ask yourself; How do you feel? Are you holding on to those feelings?

2. **Challenge Negative Thoughts*: When self-doubt arises, question the validity of your negative thoughts. Are they based on facts or assumptions?

3. **Positive Affirmations*: Counter negative self-talk with positive affirmations. Remind yourself of your strengths and accomplishments. Use your declarations to keep you focused.

4. **Celebrate Achievements:* Acknowledge and celebrate your successes, no matter how minor they seem. It reinforces your belief in your abilities. Break your task into smaller steps making progress more achievable, because an overwhelming task can fuel self-doubt. Set achievable, realistic goals, success breeds confidence, so start with small steps and build from there. Reward Yourself!!!

5. **Seek Feedback*: Ask for constructive feedback from trusted friends, mentors, or colleagues to gain a more objective perspective on your skills and abilities.

6. **Focus on Progress, Not Perfection**: Perfectionism can fuel self-doubt. Concentrate on making progress rather than aiming for perfection.

7. **Self-Compassion, Mediation and Mindfulness**: Treat yourself with kindness and understanding, just as you would a friend. Remember that everyone makes mistakes and faces challenges. Your meditation practices can help you stay present and reduce anxiety, making it easier to manage self-doubt. Ensure you get enough rest, eat healthily, and exercise regularly. Physical well-being can influence your mental state.

8. **Visualize Success**: Use visualization techniques to imagine yourself succeeding in various situations. This can boost your confidence and reduce self-doubt. Create a journal where you record your achievements and positive feedback from others. Review it when self-doubt arises.

9. **Surround Yourself with Positivity**: Spend time with people who support and uplift you. Avoid toxic relationships that feed self-doubt. Read books, watch movies, or follow individuals who inspire you. Their stories can boost your confidence completely.

10. **Learn from Failure**: Instead of seeing failure as a reflection of your abilities, view it as an opportunity to learn and grow.

11. **Take Risks:** Stepping out of your comfort zone can be uncomfortable but also empowering. Embrace challenges and learn from each one of them.

12. **Limit Comparisons**: Avoid comparing yourself to others. Everyone has their unique journey, and comparisons can breed self-doubt.

13. **Professional Help**: If self-doubt is severely impacting your life, consider seeking the guidance of a therapist or counselor who specializes in self-esteem and confidence.

Remember that self-doubt is a common human experience, and it's something that can be managed and overcome with time and effort. Be patient with yourself as you work to build your self-confidence and diminish self-doubt.

A Roadmap to Resilience:

Self-doubt is conquerable terrain. Bask in self-compassion, harness your past, champion individuality, and ignite a self-trust revolution. Through relentless introspection and empowering alliances, eradicate self-doubt's clutches. Be the architect of your self-belief, sculpting a future anchored in certainty. As you step forward, remember self-doubt is a chapter, not your story. Your narrative unfurls with each act of self-trust, fortifying your identity's foundation.
A reminder: *"I AM A CONQUEROR"*

INHALE CONFIDENCE, EXHALE DOUBT

INHALE CONFIDENCE, EXHALE DOUBT

Discovery Journey: *"Your life's purpose"*

Unveiling the profound essence of your life's purpose is a transformative journey that beckons your attention. It is a voyage of self-discovery that transcends the mundane and elevates your existence to extraordinary heights. Brace yourself for a soul-stirring expedition into the very core of your being, where your purpose resides, waiting to be unearthed.

**Soulful Self-Reflection: Set aside the chaos of daily life and delve deep within. Contemplate your passions, interests, and values with the intensity of a philosopher pondering the cosmos. Recall those moments when your heart danced with joy and pride, when you felt an inexplicable resonance with the universe. These are the clues, the whispers of your purpose.

**The Symphony of Strengths: Listen closely to the symphony of your strengths, talents, and skills. Like a maestro orchestrating a masterpiece, identify the notes that come naturally to you. Your purpose may well be the composition that utilizes these talents to create a harmonious world.

**Unearth Your Values: In the sanctum of your soul, uncover the sacred tablets of your core values and beliefs. What truths do you hold dear? Your purpose is the canvas upon which you paint your life's masterpiece, aligning every stroke with these cherished principles.

**The Flames of Passion: Fan the flames of your passions until they burn brightly, illuminating your path. What pursuits could you immerse yourself in for hours, your spirit untouched by weariness? Your purpose is nestled within these flames, waiting to ignite your journey.

Impactful Intentions: Cast your gaze upon the world and envision the impact you wish to imprint upon it. Whether in your community, within an industry, or on a global stage, define the change you aspire to create. Your purpose is the vessel that carries this transformative vision.

Bonds and Bridges: Reflect upon the bonds you cherish and the communities that resonate with your soul. Sometimes, purpose emerges from the tapestry of relationships we weave and the support we offer to others.

Conqueror of Challenges: Contemplate the crucible of adversity you've traversed. Often, these trials are signposts pointing toward a purpose rooted in helping others surmount similar challenges.

The Quest for Discovery: Do not shrink from exploring uncharted territories. Your purpose may emerge unexpectedly, born from the crucible of new experiences and opportunities. Engage in the symphony of service through volunteer work or contributions to causes close to your heart. This hands-on experience will reveal the depth of your passion and commitment to a specific purpose.

Inspirational Icons: Seek inspiration from those who have walked a path you admire. What facets of their lives and work ignite the fires of your ambition? These mentors offer glimpses into potential purposes that may suit you.

Alchemy of Passion and Proficiency: This can be compared to an artist discovering their true medium. When you seek the point where your passions and skills converge, you can uncover a purpose that is deeply satisfying and carries a significant impact, much like an artist finding their authentic form of artistic expression.

**Seek Wisdom from the Mirrors: Ask friends, family, and colleagues to reveal the brilliance they see in you. Often, they hold mirrors reflecting facets of your purpose you might overlook.

**Embrace the Winds of Change: Understand that your purpose is a living entity, capable of evolution. As you grow and experience life's ebbs and flows, your purpose may shift. Welcome this transformation. Pay heed to the whispers of your intuition, for sometimes, a silent voice guides you toward your purpose, like a compass navigating the sea of life.

**Practice the Art of Patience: Be patient, not just with the world but also with yourself. Discovering your life's purpose is a symphony that unfolds in its own time. The answers need not arrive all at once.

In your quest, remember that your purpose is unique, like a singular melody in the grand symphony of existence. Seek guidance from mentors and life coaches if the path appears convoluted. Understand that purpose, like life itself, is a journey, not a destination. Allow yourself the luxury of time and exploration, and trust that self-discovery will unveil a purpose as majestic and profound as the universe itself. Stay on this path, and soon you shall bask in the radiant glow of a purposeful life.
A reminder: *"I AM WORTHY"*

INHALE CONFIDENCE, EXHALE DOUBT

Navigating Life's Journey: *"Staying engaged with your true self"*

In the grand tapestry of existence, finding one's purpose and direction is akin to navigating through a dense forest. Each twist and turn presents choices, some seemingly leading to enlightenment, others to uncertainty. But amidst the complexity, it's crucial to remember one thing: it's perfectly acceptable, even essential, to be a tad selfish with your time and energy. Yes, you read it right. We all harbor needs and desires, facets of our being that clamor for fulfillment. Amidst the cacophony of long-term goals and grand visions for our lives, these personal inclinations must not be neglected. In fact, they should take precedence.

Even in the short term, you must allow yourself the luxury of relaxation, recovery, and self-renewal. A life wholly dedicated to fulfilling others' needs is a recipe for eventual harm and dissatisfaction. So, how do we strike this delicate balance? How do we remain steadfast on our chosen path without succumbing to the ever-present temptation of losing ourselves in the complexities of life? Let's explore this essential inquiry, offering a treasure trove of insights and strategies.

1. Practice Self-Care: *Prioritizing Your Inner Sanctuary*
In the grand theater of life, where you juggle roles and responsibilities, remember this vital act: the act of self-care. Prioritize your physical, emotional, spiritual, and mental wellbeing. It's akin to the airline safety protocol where you're instructed to don the oxygen mask on yourself before aiding others. In everyday existence, this principle remains steadfast – you must start with yourself before you can be all that others need. Consider it a personal creed, a reminder that you, too, are deserving of your own attention.

2. Practice Gratitude: *The Magic of the Present*
In our ceaseless pursuit of future milestones, we often forget the present's enchantment. The remedy? Cultivate the magic of gratitude. It's a mindfulness practice that enables you to appreciate the here and now while keeping your aspirations in perspective.

3. Stay True to Yourself: *The Compass of Authenticity*
The journey to self-discovery begins with understanding your values, passions, and strengths. These are your North Star. Align your choices with them. If you don't feel it or believe in it, then it doesn't belong in your journey.

4. Create a Vision: *Sketch the Map of Your Future*
An exciting voyage demands a vision. Envision where you aspire to be and chart your course towards it. Keep your vision ever-present by crafting a vision board; seeing it makes it palpable, almost touchable.

5. Learn Continuously: *Broading the Horizons*
The world is a vast classroom, and every day presents an opportunity to learn. Keep expanding your knowledge and skills to remain engaged and relevant. Action fuels a growth mindset.

6. Embrace Change: *The Symphony of Adaptation*
Life's melodies are ever-changing. Be open to adaptation and evolution rather than resisting change. It's just like if you started a new job, it requires you to adjust to a new environment, colleagues, and responsibilities. Just as a river flows, around an obstacle, so must you adapt to life's twists and turns.

7. Maintain a Routine: *The Cadence of Clarity*
In the chaos of existence, routines provide structure and stability. Your routine need not be mundane; it must, however, be consistent, bringing clarity and focus to your life. Effective management of time will ensure that daily responsibilities are met, including chores, appointments, and errands.

8. Surround Yourself with Positivity: *The Company You Keep*
In this grand expedition, the companions you choose matter. Surround yourself with individuals who uplift and support you, for in their eyes, you may see the specialness you sometimes overlook.
I connected with some friends that I haven't spoken to in a while, but these are friends that wherever we left off is exactly where we'll pick up, not missing a beat.

9. Practice Mindfulness: *The Art of Presence*
Instead of dwelling on my past or worrying about my future, I stay present and mindful, connecting my heart with my feelings. My gratitude shifts my thinking and responses. I've now discovered my true power in the present.

10. Reflect Regularly: *Illuminating the Path*
Regular introspection is akin to illuminating your path with a torch. Take time to reflect on your journey's progress and make necessary adjustments, always nurturing a positive perspective. Write out the positive changes taking place in your life.

11. Disconnect Regularly: *Reconnecting with Your Essence*
Amidst the digital cacophony, take breaks to reconnect with yourself and the world around you. Sometimes, silence speaks loudest.
I have learned to surround myself with uplifting books, articles and quotes that provide positivity and motivation, this practice keeps me grounded.

12. Engage in Creative Expression: <u>*The Symphony of Self-Discovery*</u>

Whether it's through art, writing, music, or any creative outlet, express yourself and in the process, you'll uncover layers of self-discovery. Through the strokes of a paintbrush or the rhythm of your words, it will often unlock the door to your innermost thoughts and feelings. Personally, I've welcomed change into my life through enrolling in a dance class and delving into the world of pottery.

These experiences have led me into uncharted territory, ultimately resulting in a profound sense of fulfillment.

13. Seek Solitude: <u>*Conversations with Your Inner Self*</u>

Alone time isn't a solitary journey into loneliness; it's a chance for deep conversations with your inner thoughts and emotions. Remember to prioritize yourself. There are numerous ways to seek solitude, and one of my personal favorites is when I indulge in a foot bath soak. It's an incredible state of relaxation that allows me to reconnect with myself.

14. Practice Assertiveness: <u>*Your Voice in the Choir*</u>

To stay true to your path, communicate your needs and desires clearly and respectfully. Let your voice be heard in the chorus of existence. In a world often pressuring conformity, maintain your authenticity. Be genuine and true to your values. Your uniqueness is your strength!

Celebrate your achievements give yourself a toast to triumph! Acknowledge, and celebrate your successes, regardless of their size. Every note in your composition matters, and every achievement deserves applause.

Remember, the path to self-discovery is a perpetual journey; a winding road that may, at times, appear as an enigmatic maze. Yet, this path is yours alone. Avoid the temptation of comparing it to others. Instead, focus on your growth, of your unique journey. In the blueprints of your day, week, month, or year, always ensure that 'you' are at the forefront. You are worthy, and your voyage is a testament to the beauty of individuality. Cherish it, nurture it, and let it illuminate your path.

A reminder: ***"I AM VALUABLE"***

INHALE CONFIDENCE, EXHALE DOUBT

Unleash Your Inner Power: *"The art of showing up"*

Imagine a life where you wake up every morning feeling invincible, where your mere presence commands respect, and where your influence can spark positive change. Such a life isn't reserved for the chosen few; it's a life that anyone can create through a powerful combination of personal development, mindset, your imagination, leadership skills, and the art of showing up. The journey to becoming a powerful person starts with the most potent weapon you possess: your mind-set. I have come to learn it's extremely important to feed the mind the correct nutrients to forge forward daily. We'll explore how you can cultivate the power of your mindset that will enable you to show up as your most authentic self and harness your inner power.

The foundation of any powerful individual is self-awareness. It's about understanding your strengths, acknowledging your weaknesses, and having a clear vision of your values and goals.
When you truly know yourself, you can make decisions that align with your authentic self, propelling you toward success with unwavering confidence. Imagine a world where you navigate decisions effortlessly because you are in tune with your true self. Your actions become more purposeful, and your life begins to take on a deeper meaning.

Confidence is the fuel that powers your journey. It's the belief in yourself and your abilities that radiates outward, attracting respect and opportunities like a magnet. Visualize when you stride into any room with the assurance that you belong, that your voice matters. This confidence is what separates the powerful from the rest.

When I enter a room, I hold my head high and smile from within and it shines brightly on my face, and nothing can change the feeling I'm experiencing at that moment.
Your bridge to Influence others is powerful, but you must master the art of communication. This involves not only expressing your thoughts clearly but also listening actively and empathetically.

Effective communication is the bridge that connects you to others, enhances your influence and amplifies your impact. Now, imagine the power of being able to sway opinions, inspire action, and build lasting relationships through your words and efforts. Knowing and understanding your emotional intelligence; is the cornerstone of strong relationships and effective conflict resolution. It's about managing your own emotions and understanding the feelings of others. Connection is currency and your ability to empathize, unite, and navigate emotions will set you apart.

Think about the advantage of fostering deep, meaningful relationships, and resolving conflicts with grace and understanding bringing harmony to your situation every time. This can be done, and you can do it!

How strong is your support system? Because no one succeeds alone. When building a diverse network of relationships this will provide you with support, resources, and opportunities. These connections can be the steppingstones to your success. Picture a life where you have a vast network of allies who believe in your vision and are willing to help you achieve it, the skies the limit.

Life is filled with challenges, but your ability to bounce back from setbacks and failures is a testament to your strength and determination. Resilience is the hallmark of powerful individuals.

Imagine facing adversity with unwavering courage, always emerging from the storm stronger and wiser. Building your problem-solving skills becomes second nature, and your ability to find answers in the midst of uncertainty adds to your power. Each time I conquer one of life's challenges, I feel like I've been given yet another gold star... you know the kind you use to get in kindergarten, they were so big to me, and I've always held on to that awesome feeling of happiness.

It's time for you to start thinking beyond your limits. Your innovation is the spark that ignites progress in life. By embracing creativity and thinking outside the box, you set yourself apart from the crowd. It's your time to push boundaries, creating groundbreaking ideas, and leave an indelible mark on the world. You have the power to guide others to greatness, your true power isn't about control; it's about inspiring and guiding others toward a common goal. When you have effective leadership, its rewards come with respect and loyalty. Envision leading a team where every member is motivated, empowered, and working together to achieve greatness. This team could be at work or home.

A positive attitude filled with gratefulness is your secret weapon. It helps you maintain optimism even in the toughest situations. I teach my grandchildren about the power of gratefulness and how it can change your life and the ones around you. Positivity attracts others and fosters a productive environment. Imagine radiating positivity, uplifting those around you, and creating a world filled with optimism and hope. Work your charisma, it is the art of exuding confidence, warmth, and authenticity.
It's a magnetic presence that draws people to you effortlessly. Like the power of captivating the room, leaving a lasting impression on everyone you meet. It's your catalyst for success.

Mentorship, both as a mentor and a mentee, accelerates your growth and influence. It's a powerful exchange of wisdom, experience, and knowledge. Visualize mentors who guide you and the satisfaction of passing on your wisdom to others, propelling them to greatness. I frequently emphasize the idea that knowledge holds power, but it's true strength emerges when shared to empower others. I abide by this principle in how I lead my life.

Planning for success through strategic thinking means looking ahead and making decisions that align with your long-term goals. It involves having a broader perspective and selecting actions that will shape the future you desire. Envision a life where your present actions are thoughtfully designed to construct the life you aspire to have in the days to come. In a world that's in constant flux, adaptability becomes your trusted companion. Picture not only surviving in the face of change but flourishing within it, using every shift as an opportunity for growth and achievement.

This journey leads to the creation of a Legacy of Impact. Remember, true power is not solely about personal gain; it's also about utilizing your influence to better the world. By contributing to causes that matter to you, you'll magnify your impact and leave behind a legacy of positive change. Never underestimate the significance of giving back and the profound effect it will have on others.

A Reminder: ***"I AM CONFIDENT"***

INHALE CONFIDENCE, EXHALE DOUBT

Setting Yourself Free: *"No turning back"*

As mothers, we often find ourselves caught in the whirlwind of responsibilities and duties, wearing multiple hats as we navigate through the maze of daily life. We become so consumed by the needs of our families that we often forget to nurture our own selves. Yet, buried beneath the layers of motherhood lies a woman with dreams, aspirations, and a unique purpose waiting to be rediscovered.

Setting yourself free from the constraints of societal expectations and the self-imposed limitations is the first step towards reclaiming your identity. It's about recognizing that you are more than just a caregiver, a chef, a chauffeur, or a mediator. You are a multifaceted individual with talents, passions, and desires that deserve to be acknowledged and nurtured.

Rediscovering who you are and your purpose for life requires a journey inward, a journey of self-reflection and introspection. It's about peeling back the layers of conditioning and expectations to uncover the essence of your true self. What are your passions? What brings you joy and fulfillment? What legacy do you want to leave behind?

There is no turning back to who you used to be, for you have evolved and grown through your experiences. You are no longer the same person you were before and that's okay. Embrace the woman you have become, with all her imperfections and vulnerabilities, for she is beautiful and worthy of love and acceptance.

Lost amongst all the many titles you carry in life, it's easy to lose sight of your own needs and desires. But now is the time to reclaim your power and prioritize yourself. It's about striking a balance between nurturing your family and nurturing yourself, knowing that you cannot pour from an empty cup.

Changing your mindset is key to unlocking the door to personal freedom and fulfillment. Instead of viewing your many titles as a burden or sacrifice, see it as an opportunity for growth and self-discovery. Look at the world through a different lens, one that celebrates your strengths and embraces your uniqueness.

Realize that this world is a place you like, a place where you can thrive and flourish, not just survive. It's about finding joy in the little moments, savoring the beauty of everyday life, and cherishing the connections that nourish your soul.

Although you love your family to life and they will always be a priority, the difference now is that so will you. You are no longer content to be just a supporting character in your own story. You are the protagonist, the heroine of your own journey, and it's time to reclaim your power and rewrite your narrative.

So, My Love, set yourself free from the chains of self-doubt and insecurity. Embrace your authentic self and step into the fullness of who you are meant to be. Rediscover your purpose, reignite your passions, and know that the best is yet to come. There is no turning back, only forward, towards a life filled with meaning, fulfillment, and limitless possibilities. So, until next time continue to be **"PHENOMENAL"**

INHALE CONFIDENCE, EXHALE DOUBT

Key Words to Live By:

As you embark on your journey to unleash your inner power, keep these words in your heart and mind:

I AM:

Worthy, Strong, Grateful, Courageous, Confident, Smart, Resilient, Adventurous, Deserving, Positive, Brave, Empowered, Creative, Powerful, Beautiful, Encouraging, Phenomenal, Determined, Inspirational, Dedicated, Ambitious, Considerate, Funny, Happy and Loved.

These words aren't just descriptors; they are affirmations of your potential and reminders of the person you are becoming. Make them a part of your daily declarations and watch as they transform your life. So, get ready to embark on a journey of self-discovery, growth, and empowerment, where you'll learn to flex your power and truly show up in every aspect of your life.
A reminder: *"I AM INCREDIBLE"*

INHALE CONFIDENCE, EXHALE DOUBT

Just a little something...

Staying present amidst the chaos requires a conscious effort to ground yourself in the current moment. It involves acknowledging the multitude of titles we carry but not letting them define our entire existence. The key to navigating this complexity is to never lose sight of who you are. Amidst the chaos, it's crucial to reconnect with your core values, passions, and aspirations. This self-awareness serves as your anchor, ensuring you don't compromise your authenticity for the sake of fulfilling societal or personal expectations. Remembering your purpose in life becomes a guiding light, providing direction and meaning to your journey.

Maintaining gratitude in the face of challenges is a powerful tool for cultivating resilience. Life's circumstances may vary but finding the silver lining and appreciating the positive aspects, no matter how small, can significantly impact your perspective. Gratitude becomes a beacon of hope, reminding you that even in difficult times, there is a bright light ahead waiting to be discovered.
I can't stress it enough, embracing gratitude with the full intensity of your heart is the ultimate key to living and profoundly comprehending the immeasurable value of life. It's what gets me through each day, just being grateful.

To navigate the complexities of life with grace, it's essential to be fearless and advocate for yourself. This involves recognizing your worth and deservingness of a fulfilling life. Setting and enforcing your boundaries becomes a crucial aspect of self-care, ensuring that you prioritize your well-being amidst the myriad demands. It's a declaration of self-love and a commitment to maintaining a healthy balance. You can do it!

In the pursuit of staying true to yourself, embrace the phenomenal individual that you are. Celebrate your strengths, acknowledge your growth, and love every facet of your being. You are deserving of all the goodness life has to offer, and by remaining steadfast in your authenticity, you can create a life that aligns with your true essence. Stay present, stay grateful, and above all, be fearless in the pursuit of your purpose and happiness.

XOXO ~ Your Biggest Cheerleader,
Kimberly Gail

INHALE CONFIDENCE, EXHALE DOUBT

Conclusion

This guide empowers women to "**Inhale Confidence and Exhale Doubt**" through a process of redefining their lives offers a transformative journey towards self-discovery and empowerment. By addressing the deep-seated issues of self-doubt and insecurity, this guide provides women with practical tools and insights to cultivate a strong sense of confidence and self-worth.

The guide emphasizes the importance of self-awareness as a foundation for change. Through introspective exercises and reflection, you are encouraged to identify the sources of their doubts and recognize how the limiting beliefs have shaped your life. By confronting these negative thought patterns, you can begin the process of reshaping your self-perception.

Redefining one's life involves setting new and empowering narratives. The guide offers guidance on goal setting, self-compassion, and the practice of positive affirmations. By embracing their strengths, accomplishments, and unique qualities, you can gradually replace doubt with a genuine sense of confidence.

The guide also stresses the significance of community and support. I encouraged you to surround yourself with uplifting individuals who believe in your potential. This may consist of group discussions, mentoring, and networking can play a pivotal role in boosting confidence and fostering a sense of belonging.

While the journey to inhaling confidence and exhaling doubt may not be linear, the guide underscores the importance of perseverance and self-care. It acknowledges that setbacks and moments of self-doubt are natural, but with the tools provided, women can navigate these challenges and continue on their path to self-empowerment.

I'm offering a comprehensive roadmap for women to overcome self-doubt and cultivate genuine confidence by redefining their lives. Through self-awareness, positive affirmations, goal setting, and community engagement, women can embark on a transformative journey that leads to a more empowered and fulfilled existence.

By embracing the principles outlined in the guide, women have the opportunity to rewrite their stories and embrace their authentic selves with newfound confidence.
"CHALLENGE TO PUT YOURSELF FIRST!"

INHALE CONFIDENCE, EXHALE DOUBT

"If you don't define who you are…
the world will have
no problem
stepping in and
doing it for you."

Take Control!

YOU ARE:

WHOLE, PERFECT, STRONG, POWERFUL, LOVING, HARMONIOUS and HAPPY!

~ Charles F. Haanel

NOW IS THE TIME...

Have you ever stopped to think about the incredible power that resides within you? It's a force that can move mountains, change lives, and shape destinies. It's the power of your purpose, waiting to be unlocked and unleashed.

Your mindset is the key that can open the doors to a world of possibility. It's about believing in yourself, your dreams, and the impact you can have on this world. It's about realizing that your purpose is not just a distant dream, but a tangible reality waiting for you to embrace it. So, take a moment to reflect on your incredible journey. Embrace the power within you, change your mindset, and watch as your purpose unfolds before your eyes. You are powerful, you are purposeful, and you have the potential to make a difference like no one else.

KIMBERLY GAIL SAUNDERS, is a speaker, thought leader, confidence coach, author, and CEO of "MOM'S WINNING 1," who devotes her energies to helping mothers who have lost their path amidst the multitude of roles they play in life. Guiding them on a voyage of self-awakening to embrace their true selves, enabling them to shine brighter than ever before.

Visit Website:

www.KimberlyGailspeaks.com

INHALE CONFIDENCE, EXHALE DOUBT

Made in the USA
Middletown, DE
25 March 2025

73199421R10050